FIRST 15 LESSONS

UKULELE

by Michael Ezra

T0039563

**Includes Audio
& Video Access**

PLAYBACK+
Speed • Pitch • Balance • Loop

To access audio, video, and extra content visit:
www.halleonard.com/mylibrary

Enter Code
3811-6954-7797-3354

ISBN 978-1-5400-2073-4

HAL•LEONARD®

Contact Us:
Hal Leonard
7777 West Bluemound Road
Milwaukee, WI 53213
Email: info@halleonard.com

In Europe contact:
Hal Leonard Europe Limited
42 Wigmore Street
Marylebone, London, W1U 2RN
Email: info@halleonardeurope.com

In Australia contact:
Hal Leonard Australia Pty. Ltd.
4 Lentara Court
Cheltenham, Victoria, 3192 Australia
Email: info@halleonard.com.au

UKULELE ANATOMY AND SIZES

Ukulele anatomy refers to the different parts that make up the instrument. The photo below shows a basic soprano-sized ukulele with each part clearly labeled. Learning the names of these parts can help you communicate with others when discussing the uke—whether it be with a salesman at a music shop or with a fellow player.

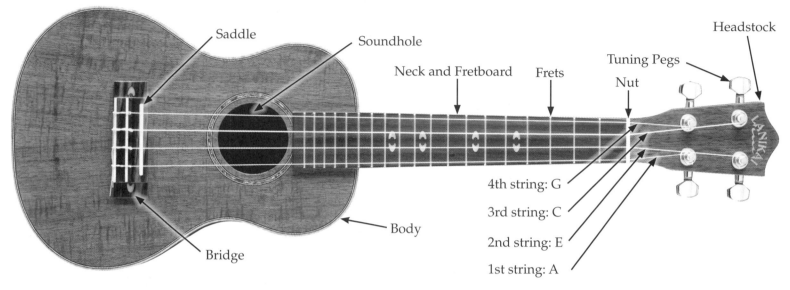

Saddle · Soundhole · Neck and Fretboard · Frets · Nut · Tuning Pegs · Headstock · Body · Bridge

4th string: G
3rd string: C
2nd string: E
1st string: A

Ukuleles come in four main sizes. Ranging from smallest to largest, these are *soprano* (or "standard"), *concert*, *tenor*, and *baritone*. They're all tuned to the same pitches, except for the baritone, which is lower in pitch. The soprano has the "brightest," or "tinniest," sound, whereas the baritone has the most full-bodied, or "bassy," sound. If you haven't yet purchased a uke, go to a store and try them out to see which one feels best.

> **NOTE:** The music in this book is designed for a soprano, concert, or tenor ukulele. If you have a baritone uke, it won't sound the same as the audio and video.

TUNING THE UKULELE

There are many ways to tune the ukulele, such as electronic tuners, tuning apps, and online tuners.

> A free online tuner comes with this book! Simply visit **www.halleonard.com/mylibrary** and enter the code found on page 1 to access it.

Once you have a tuner on hand, you can begin tuning each of the four strings. Here are the pitches of the open strings, from string 4 (nearest to the ceiling) to string 1 (nearest to the floor): G–C–E–A

Ukuleles are tuned in what's called *reentrant tuning*. This means that string 4, which would normally be the lowest pitch on an instrument with four strings, is actually tuned higher in pitch than string 2. In fact, its pitch is just below string 1. Reentrant tuning is largely responsible for the ukulele's signature sound. Twisting the tuning keys clockwise will lower the pitches of the strings, while turning them counterclockwise will raise the pitches. As you pluck a string, twist the corresponding tuning key until the tuner's meter matches the desired pitch.

HOLDING THE UKULELE

The ukulele can be played standing or sitting and with or without a strap. The pictures below illustrate proper sitting and standing posture. If you're not using a strap, cradle the instrument against your ribs with the forearm of your strumming hand.

with strap

without strap

STRUMMING AND PLUCKING

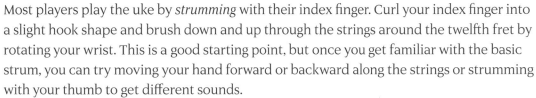

Most players play the uke by *strumming* with their index finger. Curl your index finger into a slight hook shape and brush down and up through the strings around the twelfth fret by rotating your wrist. This is a good starting point, but once you get familiar with the basic strum, you can try moving your hand forward or backward along the strings or strumming with your thumb to get different sounds.

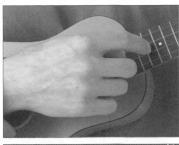

You can also use your thumb and fingers to pluck the strings of your uke. To use this technique, which is called *fingerpicking*, place your thumb on string 4, index on string 3, middle on string 2, and ring finger on string 1, near the soundhole, as a starting point. Try plucking the individual strings one at a time using these fingers. Once you get the hang of it, you can try moving your plucking fingers to different strings, depending on the musical phrase you're playing at the time.

UKULELE TAB, CHORD FRAMES, AND RHYTHM SLASHES

In place of standard notation, we're going to use *tab* (short for "tablature") throughout this book. Tab uses numbers, which represent the frets of the ukulele, instead of notes. And unlike the standard five-line musical staff, ukulele tab has four horizontal lines, each representing a string on the ukulele. Specifically, we'll use *rhythm tab*, which will convey the rhythm of each note as well as the pitch. (We'll learn about rhythms in Lesson 2.)

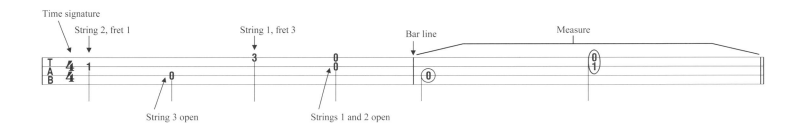

In addition to tab, we will be using *chord diagrams*, or *chord frames*. These represent "snapshots" of the ukulele neck—as if you were holding it directly in front of you rather than looking down at it while in playing position. The vertical lines represent the four strings, while the horizontal lines indicate frets.

Black dots indicate finger placement, and the numbers below the frames indicate which fingers to use: 1 = index, 2 = middle, 3 = ring, 4 = pinky. When a curved line appears over multiple dots, those strings are to be played with a fret-hand *barre*. (You'll begin learning about barres in Lesson 6.)

These chord frames will be used in conjunction with *rhythm slashes*, which are simply a shorthand for showing strumming patterns:

3

4/4 TIME

Most music you'll encounter is written in *4/4 time* (or *meter*), which is also known as "common time." Each number in the fraction, known as the *time signature*, represents a rhythmic component. The top number tells you how many beats are in each *measure*, or *bar* (vertical lines, or *bar lines*, in the staff divide the music into measures); the bottom number indicates which type of rhythm is counted as one beat: 2 = half note, 4 = quarter note, and 8 = eighth note. In 4/4 time, then, there are four beats (top number = 4) per measure, and each quarter note (bottom number = 4) receives one beat.

WHOLE NOTES, HALF NOTES, AND QUARTER NOTES

Different rhythms in the music are used to indicate how long each note is played. Three common rhythms you'll find in 4/4 time are whole notes, half notes, and quarter notes. As we discussed earlier, there are four beats per measure in 4/4 time. Keeping that in mind, if you understand fractions, then these names make a lot of sense. A *whole note* receives four beats. In other words, it lasts the whole measure. A *half note* receives two beats, so it lasts a half measure, or half as long as a whole note. Count along—"1, 2, 3, 4," etc.—as we play these rhythms on the open third string. You can pluck the string with your thumb or index finger.

Example 1

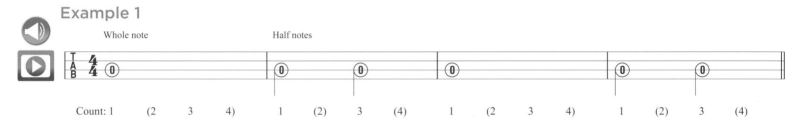

Quarter notes receive one beat, so they last a quarter of a measure, or one-fourth as long as a whole note. Let's add some quarter notes to our half and whole notes.

Example 2

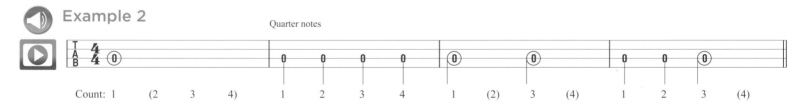

OPEN C, F, G, AND Am CHORDS

Now that we've gotten a grip on some rhythm concepts, let's take a look at our first chords. A *chord* is simply a collection of harmonious notes played at the same time. Below are the chord frames for C, F, G, and Am. These *chord symbols* stand for the chords C major, F major, G major, and A minor, respectively. Major chords sound happy or bright, whereas minor chords sound sad or dark. These are *open chords* because they incorporate at least one open (unfretted) string, unlike other fully fretted chord voicings. (A *voicing* is a particular arrangement of the notes in a chord. There is always more than one way to play a chord on the ukulele.)

Now, let's use these chords with our first three rhythms: whole notes, half notes, and quarter notes. First, we'll play whole notes on each chord, then switch to half notes, and so on. Be sure to count as you play. It's highly recommended that you use a *metronome*—a time-keeping device—when playing through these examples.

A free online tuner comes with this book! Simply visit **www.halleonard.com/mylibrary**
and enter the code found on page 1 to access it.

Before you dive in, here are a few chord tips to keep in mind:

1. Notice which strings should be fretted and which strings should be played open (O).
2. Try picking each string individually first. Make necessary finger adjustments (shifts, pressing harder, etc.) if any strings sound muted or aren't ringing clearly.
3. When fretting a note, place your finger just behind the fret as opposed to the middle area between frets. Don't move too far back from the fret, because the note won't sound clearly.
4. Long fingernails (on your fret hand) aren't your friends. Fretting cleanly will be much easier if you keep them trimmed.
5. For now, strum down through each chord (toward the floor) with either your index finger or thumb.

Example 3

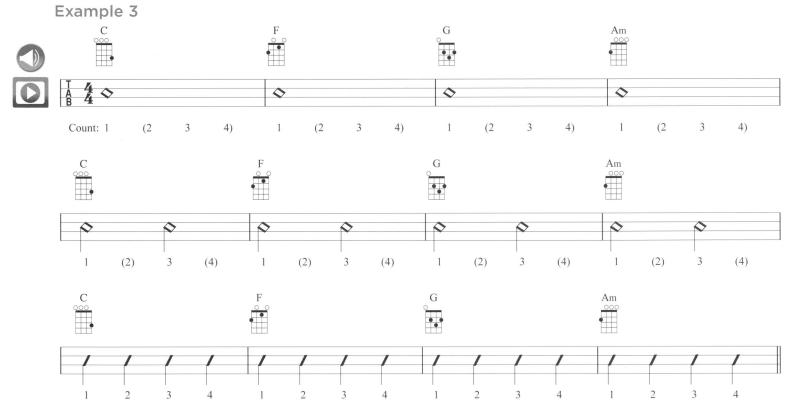

Once you feel comfortable with these four chords, try playing the following two song examples. First up is the classic Beatles tune "Let It Be." We'll use all four chords here and strum mostly in quarter notes, sustaining the final chord for a half note. When playing slowly like this, try strumming down with your thumb to get a bigger, lusher sound.

"Let It Be"

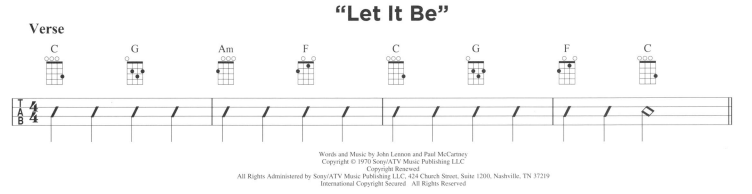

Now, let's try the '80s hit "Centerfold," by the J. Geils Band. We're using G, F, and C chords here, mixing half notes and quarter notes. Be careful with the F chord! We're playing it for only one beat, so you have to be quick with that chord change.

"Centerfold"

RESTS

Just as we have ways to notate notes and chords in music, we also need to notate silences. This is where *rests* come in. For every note rhythm (whole note, half note, etc.), there is a corresponding rest symbol that indicates silence for a specific duration.

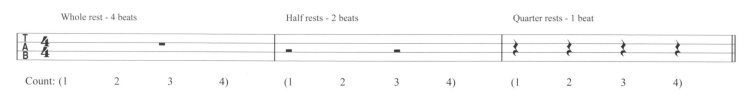

Whenever you see a rest in the music, you need to stop your uke from ringing. This is best accomplished by either laying a fret-hand finger across all the strings or laying your strumming hand down on the strings. Both methods may be used, depending on context.

OPEN D AND A CHORDS

Before we try out our rests, let's learn two more major chords: D and A. First up is D major, which can be a bit tricky—especially on a soprano uke—as it requires you to cram three fingers into the space of one fret. Try all the suggested fingerings to see which works best for you.

Now, let's try the A major chord. This is a relative of the Am chord you learned in Lesson 2. Notice that the only difference between the two chords is the note on string 3. For Am, string 3 is played open; for A, it's played at fret 1.

So let's put these two new chords to work in an exercise with some rests. Be sure to count along. For the rests, just lay your strumming hand on the strings while you re-fret for the next chord.

Example 1

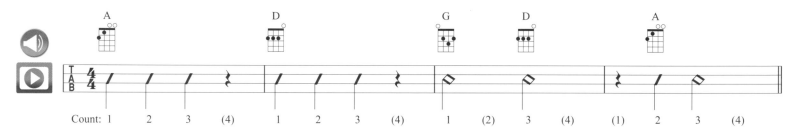

Now, let's take a look at the chorus from Bachman-Turner Overdrive's "You Ain't Seen Nothin' Yet." We'll use G, D, and C chords with some rests for a dramatic sound. You have only one beat to move from D to C, so you may want to experiment with different fingerings for the D and C chords to see which make the transition easiest. (Note: We already looked at some fingering alternatives for the D chord; for the C chord, experiment with using your pinky to fret the third fret of the first string.)

"You Ain't Seen Nothin' Yet"

OPEN F#M CHORD

The F#m (read as "F-sharp minor") chord is similar to the A major chord. You just need to add your ring finger at fret 2 on string 2.

The symbol ♯ is a *sharp*, and it's one of two *accidentals* you'll see in music. The other accidental you'll see is a flat ♭, which we'll cover in Lesson 9. Accidentals are the names we give for notes that fall "in between" the *natural notes* (the notes with no sharps or flats: A, B, C, D, E, F, and G).

The easiest way to think about natural notes and accidentals is by referring to the piano keyboard. The white keys are the natural notes, and the black keys are the accidentals. Basically, sharp means "one note higher," and flat means "one note lower." So, on the piano, the black key between the white C and D keys can either be called C♯ (one note higher than C) or D♭ (one note lower than D), depending on the musical context.

Let's try playing a reggae-style riff with our new F#m chord. We'll be resting on beats 1 and 3 and playing the chord on beats 2 and 4. So you'll just need to alternate between muting the strings and strumming the strings: mute–strum–mute–strum, etc. The symbols at the beginning (‖:) and end (:‖) are called *repeat signs*. They tell you to play everything enclosed within the two signs again.

Example 2

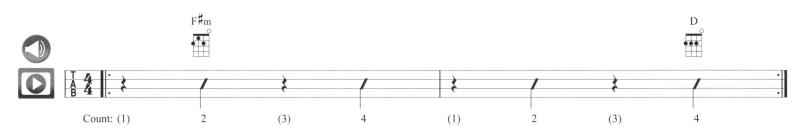

By combining our A major and F#m chords with our reggae strum, we can play Bob Marley's "Buffalo Soldier." Notice that there are dots above the quarter notes throughout. These are *staccato markings*, and they tell you to play the notes in a short, clipped manner. In other words, you would strum the chords and then immediately stop the strings from ringing.

"Buffalo Soldier"

EIGHTH NOTES

If a whole note lasts a full measure of 4/4 (four beats), a half note lasts half a measure (two beats), and a quarter note lasts one quarter of a measure (one beat), then you can most likely guess that an *eighth note* lasts one eighth of a measure, or half a beat. When counting eighth notes, we simply add an "and" (&) in between the beats. Also, notice how the eighth notes have a *beam* connecting them when they are played in groups. Let's pluck our open third string in quarter notes and then eighth notes. Be sure to count along.

Example 1

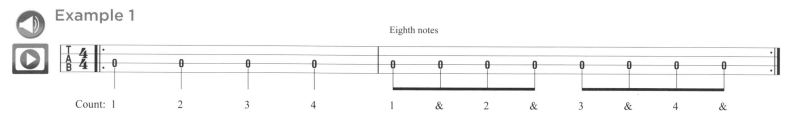

Now, let's try strumming some chords with eighth notes. Alternate between downstrums and upstrums. In other words, strum down (toward the floor) on beats 1, 2, 3, and 4. But for the "in-between" strums—i.e., the "&" strums after beats 3 and 4—strum up toward the ceiling. In the music, downstrums are indicated with a ⊓ symbol, and upstrums are indicated with V.

Example 2

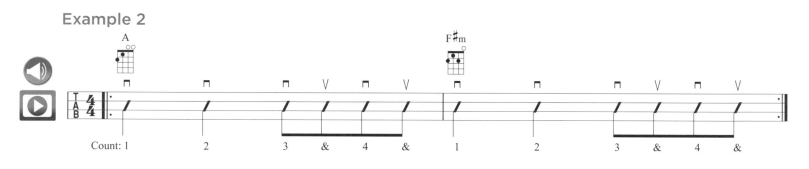

OPEN E7 CHORD

The chords we've learned so far have all been a type called triads. A *triad* is so named because it contains three different notes. On the ukulele, one of these notes will usually be doubled because we often play four-string chords, but there are still only three *different* notes.

In a *seventh chord*, there are four different notes. Our new E7 chord is a *dominant seventh chord*. And now, let's put that new chord to use in Ben E. King's "Stand by Me." The *chord progression* for this song—i.e., the order in which the chords appear—is A–F♯m–D–E7. We'll use the same strumming pattern we used in our previous exercise.

"Stand by Me"

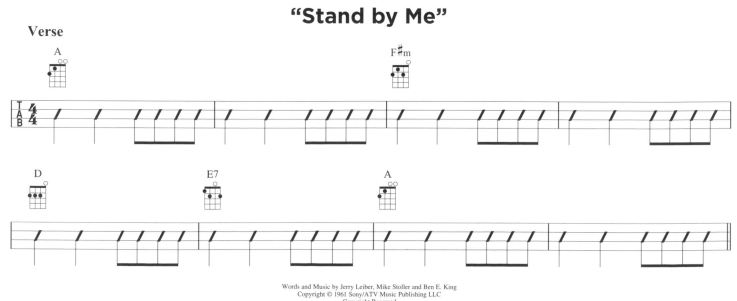

SHUFFLE FEEL

A rhythmic feel that's very common on the ukulele is the *shuffle feel*, or *swing feel*. In a shuffle feel, the eighth notes are "swung." This means that the first eighth note in each beat is longer than the second—approximately twice as long—creating a lopsided feel to the beat. You've heard this in countless songs, but it's particularly common in blues and jazz music. We'll strum a C chord in normal, or "straight," eighth notes and then again in "swung" eighth notes—i.e., with a shuffle feel, indicated by the symbol.

Example 3

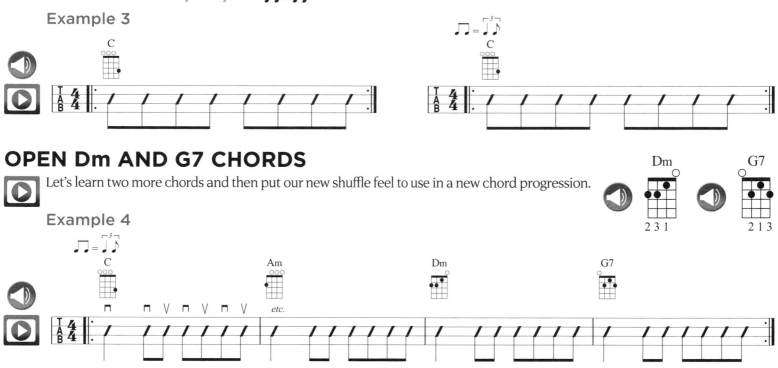

OPEN Dm AND G7 CHORDS

Let's learn two more chords and then put our new shuffle feel to use in a new chord progression.

Example 4

Now, let's gather most of the chords we've seen thus far into a song with a shuffle feel. "When I'm Sixty-Four," by the Beatles, sounds great on the uke. We'll look at the song's bridge here, which begins on an Am chord.

"When I'm Sixty-Four"

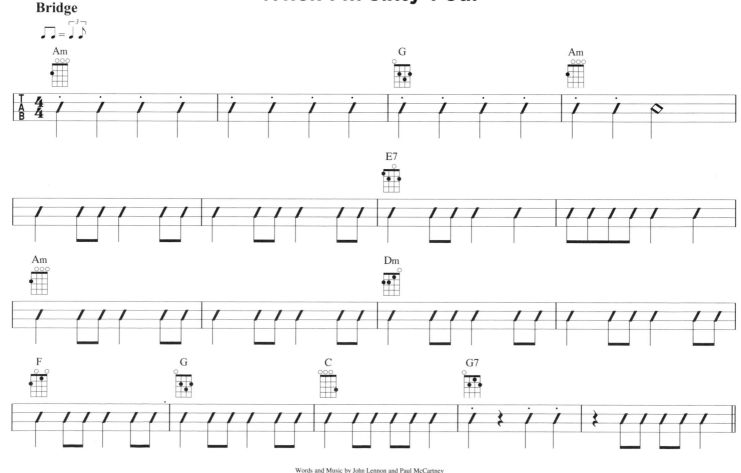

Words and Music by John Lennon and Paul McCartney
Copyright © 1967 Sony/ATV Music Publishing LLC
Copyright Renewed
All Rights Administered by Sony/ATV Music Publishing LLC, 424 Church Street, Suite 1200, Nashville, TN 37219
International Copyright Secured   All Rights Reserved

OPEN Gm AND Em CHORDS

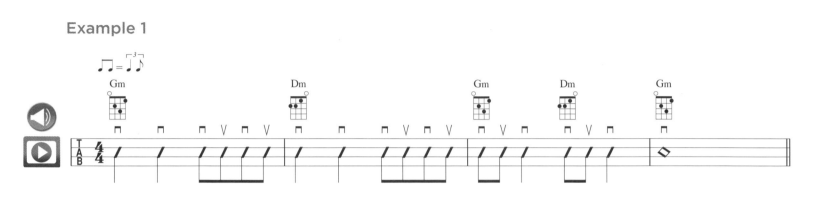

Let's add Gm and Em to our collection of minor chords. Both use three different fingers on strings 1–3 and have the fourth string open. Note that we're in *second position* for the Em chord; i.e., our first finger is on the second fret. Let's try alternating between Gm and Dm. In this example, note that the *harmonic rhythm*—the pace at which the chords change—speeds up. We start off changing chords every measure but then change twice as fast, every two beats.

Example 1

What's a Key?

When a song is said to be "in the key of A" or "in the key of C," this means that it uses a collection of chords and notes that belong to a certain "family." Each key is made up of seven different notes, or a *scale* (which we'll look at soon), and those notes are used to form melodies and chords.

For a song that's in the key of C, for example, the note C will sound like "home." In other words, the melody will feel resolved when it reaches the C note. This note is called the *tonic* (or sometimes *root*) of the key. If you're not sure what's meant by "home" or "resolved," think of the "Star Spangled Banner." What would you think if someone sang "and the home of the ..." and then just stopped? You'd wait for a second and then want to blurt out "brave!" That's because the melody wasn't resolved. The note of the word "brave" is the tonic of the key, and that's why it feels resolved when we hear it.

Let's put our new Gm and Em chords to use. This next example sounds very much like a classic song by the Doors, but it's in a different key. When the same chord progressions are played in different keys, they sound basically the same—one just sounds higher or lower than the other. (For instance, think of a baseball or hockey game where the organ plays the familiar four-note melody that starts low and keeps repeating higher each time, eventually culminating in the "Charge!" melody. This is an example of the same thing being played in a different key.)

Example 2

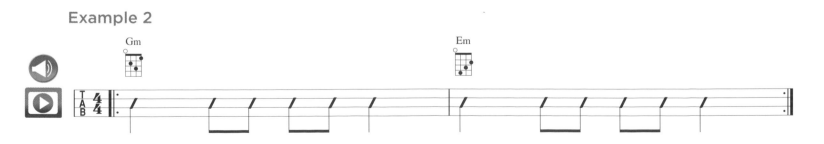

SYNCOPATION

In many strum patterns, the chords change on the *downbeat* (beat 1) of a measure, so those beats tend to feel slightly *accented*, or more pronounced, as compared to the other beats of a measure. *Syncopation*, however, means that we place an accent (emphasis) on a "weak" beat or part of a beat. Perhaps the easiest way to do this in a 4/4 pattern is to change chords on an upbeat—i.e., the "ands" between the counts—instead of on the beats (the numbers).

In practice, we hear syncopation all the time in almost every genre. Whether in the vocal melody, the chord progression, or a riff, it's usually in every song we hear. In fact, music would end up sounding pretty square if it didn't include any syncopation.

So, let's try it out with Santana's "Evil Ways," which moves between Gm and C. We're strumming with a mixture of quarter notes and eighth notes, but notice that the change to Gm happens on the upbeat every other time. This places a natural accent on that part of the beat, and thus we say that chord change is syncopated. Be sure to count along and follow the strum indications.

"Evil Ways"

Verse

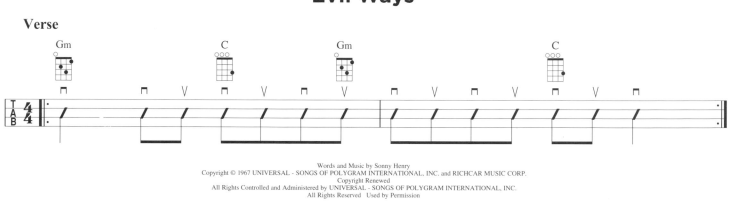

While that was a mild form of syncopation—with only one syncopated chord every other measure—the effect can certainly be more pronounced. A perfect example is the opening riff to AC/DC's "Highway to Hell." Who says ukuleles can't rock out? Take this one slowly at first and follow the strum indications closely. You may notice that there's an incomplete measure at the beginning. Those notes are called *pickup notes*, and they precede the first true downbeat of the song. When you see pickup notes, you simply start counting an imaginary measure and join in at the appropriate time. (By the way, pickup measures are not counted when numbering measures; in other words, measure 1 will be the first *complete* measure.)

"Highway to Hell"

Intro

TIES AND DOTS

A *tie* is a curved line connecting two notes (or several notes) of the same pitch. In our rhythm tab system, a dashed line is used for ties, but in standard notation or slash notation, a solid line is used. A tie tells you to combine the rhythm of the two tied notes and sustain it throughout. In other words, if a quarter note is tied to another quarter note, you'll hold the note for two beats (one beat + one beat). You'll often see ties used between measures, as in the following example. Be sure to count along in order to keep your place through the tie!

Example 1

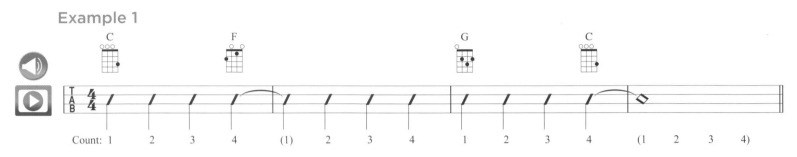

Another way to extend the duration of a note (or notes) is with a *dot*. When a dot appears to the right of a note, you extend the note's value by half its duration. So, whereas a half note lasts for two beats, a *dotted half note* lasts for three beats. Whereas a quarter note lasts for one beat, a *dotted quarter note* lasts for one-and-a-half beats, and so on. Be sure to count along with the following example, which demonstrates dotted quarter- and dotted half-note rhythms.

Example 2

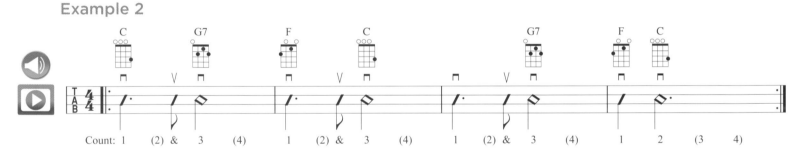

OPEN E♭ AND Cm CHORDS

Let's learn two more open chords that will prove useful when playing in certain keys. The Cm chord is our first barre chord. In a *barre chord*, we're required to lay one finger across several strings at the same fret. In this case, we're barring with our index finger at fret 3 on strings 1–3. We'll look more closely at barre chords in Lesson 7. Let's put these two chords to use in another syncopated strum pattern.

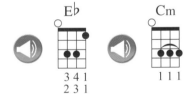

Example 3

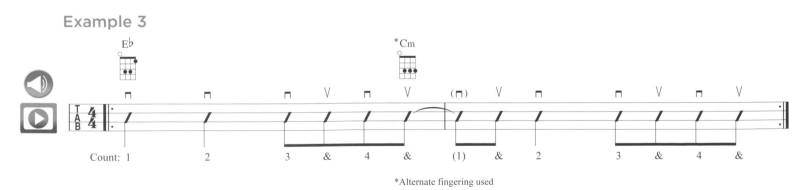

*Alternate fingering used

SUS CHORDS

Now, we'll learn another chord type: the *sus chord*. Short for "suspended," a sus chord has three different notes, just like a triad, but they're not the same three notes. The two types of sus chords we'll look at are sus2 and sus4. Unlike the triads we've looked at thus far, sus chords are neither major nor minor. We'll talk a bit more about the workings of these chords in Lesson 7.

Sus4 Chords

Let's look at a few sus4 chords first. Try alternating between each of these and their respective major and minor triads. This is, in fact, one of the most common uses of sus chords—as a decoration to or variation on a major or minor triad.

A classic sus4 chord riff is found in Tom Petty's "Free Fallin'." In this example, we'll use both Fsus4 and Csus4, as well as some dots and ties. When moving from F to Fsus4, keep your index finger on fret 1, string 2 and simply roll it over to make the necessary barre.

"Free Fallin'"

In the Police's "Roxanne," we'll make use of our new Cm and E♭ chords along with Fsus4 and Gsus4. Notice that Gsus4 appears on the "and" of beat 4 and there's an "x" note right before it on beat 4. This "x" indicates a *muted strum*, which means your fret hand should make contact with the strings without applying any pressure. This results in a deadened, percussive sound when you strum.

"Roxanne"

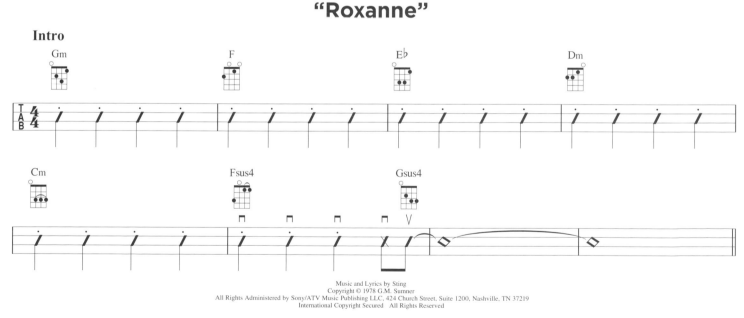

Sus2 Chords

Now, let's check out a few sus2 chords. Notice that Fsus2 alternates well with the other version of F major seen here.

FINGERPICKING ARPEGGIOS

Strumming creates a great sound on the uke, but fingerpicking is a lot of fun too; and because of the reentrant tuning, it can sound really interesting as well. To start off, plant your plucking-hand thumb, index, middle, and ring fingers on strings 4–1, respectively, near the soundhole. Your thumb should be closer to the nut and your fingers closer to the bridge. Now, pluck the strings from the fourth to the first in quarter notes. (Note: When identifying the plucking fingers, we use the following system adopted from the guitar: thumb = *p*, index = *i*, middle = *m*, and ring = *a*.)

Example 1

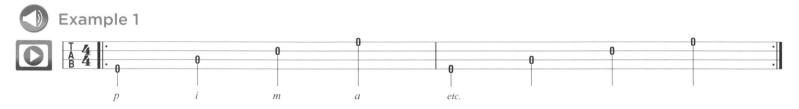

Now, let's apply the same fingerpicking pattern to a few different chords. By doing this, each chord becomes an *arpeggio*, which is a chord with its notes played individually rather than at the same time. Notice the wavy vertical line on the last C chord; this is telling you to just brush down through the strings with your thumb.

Example 2

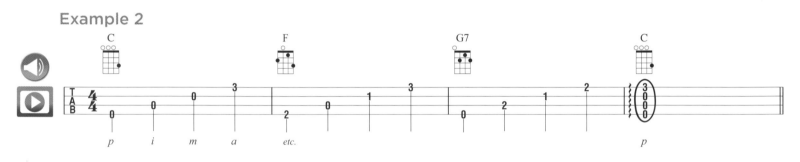

6/8 TIME

To demonstrate another common fingerpicking pattern, let's look at a time signature called 6/8. In 6/8 time, the eighth note is counted as the beat, and there are six beats in each measure. The first and fourth eighth notes in each measure are naturally accented, so 6/8 is counted as "**1**, 2, 3, **4**, 5, 6," etc. You'll notice that the beaming of the eighth notes supports this as well. In regard to fingerpicking, this makes for a nice rolling pattern of *p–i–m–a–m–i*. Let's check it out with a chord progression in D minor.

Example 3

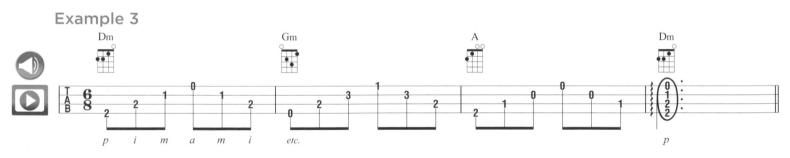

To put our 6/8 rolling fingerpicking pattern into action, let's check out the Animals' version of "The House of the Rising Sun."

"The House of the Rising Sun"

Verse

Am   C   D   F

T A B
6/8

p   i   m   a   m   i   *etc.*

Words and Music by Alan Price
Copyright © 1964 Keith Prowse Music Publishing Co., Ltd. and ole Cantaloupe Music
Copyright Renewed
All Rights Administered by Sony/ATV Music Publishing LLC, 424 Church Street, Suite 1200, Nashville, TN 37219
International Copyright Secured   All Rights Reserved

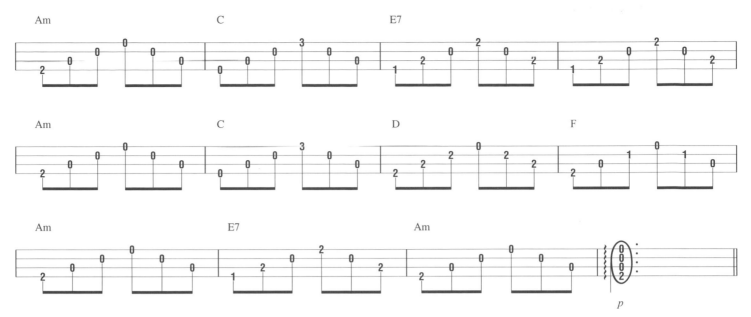

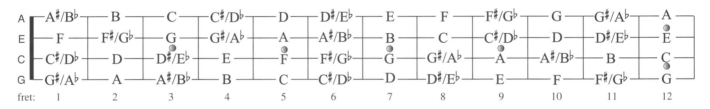

MOVABLE BARRE CHORDS

We first got our feet wet using barre chords with Cm in Lesson 6, but now we're going to dive in head first. Knowing these movable barre-chord shapes will open up a whole new world of possibilities. A *movable* chord shape is one in which there are no open strings. This means that playing the chord from a different root is as simple as sliding the shape up or down the neck to a different position. Here's a fretboard diagram that shows all the notes on the neck up to fret 12 (at which point they would start over):

	A♯/B♭	B	C	C♯/D♭	D	D♯/E♭	E	F	F♯/G♭	G	G♯/A♭	A
A												
E	F	F♯/G♭	G	G♯/A♭	A	A♯/B♭	B	C	C♯/D♭	D	D♯/E♭	E
C	C♯/D♭	D	D♯/E♭	E	F	F♯/G♭	G	G♯/A♭	A	A♯/B♭	B	C
G	G♯/A♭	A	A♯/B♭	B	C	C♯/D♭	D	D♯/E♭	E	F	F♯/G♭	G
fret:	1	2	3	4	5	6	7	8	9	10	11	12

In the following chord frames, the root note(s) are circled. You can use the above diagram as a reference when you want to play a barre shape from a different root. Simply move the shape to the position in which the circled (root) note is at the appropriate fret.

Let's first look at an A-form major barre chord. When we say "A-form," we mean that it resembles the open A major chord. If we play the open A chord using fret-hand fingers 3 and 2 instead of fingers 2 and 1, and lay our first finger behind the nut, as if it were "fretting" the open strings, then we can see the barre-chord form. If we move that shape up one fret, we have a B♭ major barre chord. (Remember, the root notes are circled in the chord frames.)

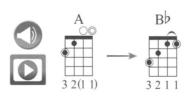

Following are movable shapes for C-form, F-form, Am-form, Dm-form, and F♯m-form chords, shown in a similar manner.

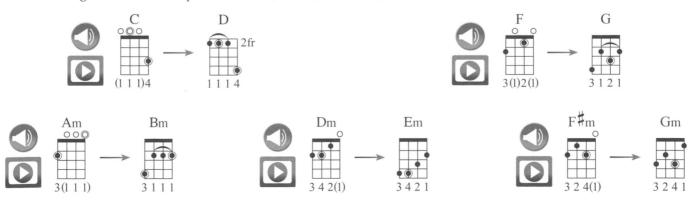

15

At this point, you know many chords and are familiar with some technical concepts such as strumming, fingerpicking, syncopation, and shuffle feel. In this lesson, we're going to put these skills to work on a full song arrangement. The Turtles had a #1 hit with "Happy Together" in 1967, and our arrangement of the song features many of the concepts we've studied thus far.

Before you get started, take note of the following:

1. The song is played with a shuffle feel.

2. You will use fingerpicking for the intro (note the plucking-hand indications). Also, the intro is based on an F♯m chord, but there are some additional notes in there as well. Take this slowly at first until you've got it steady!

3. There are some *routing directions* in the song, which are similar to repeat signs in that they save us from having to write out the same music again. When you see *D.S. al Coda,* it is telling you to go back to the D.S. symbol (𝄋) and play until you see *To Coda.* At that point, you jump to the Coda (⊕) and play on from there.

"Happy Together"

%S Chorus

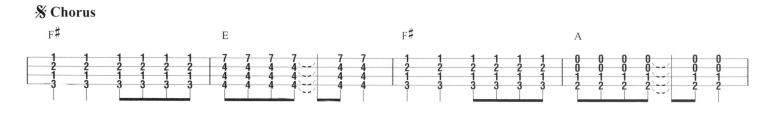

To Coda

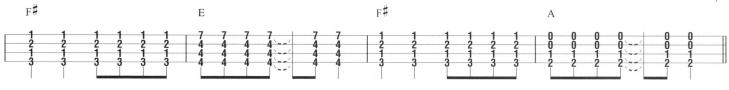

Verse

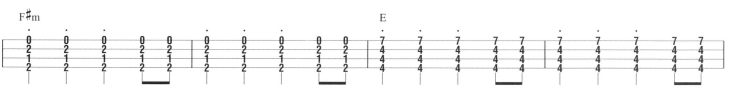

D.S. al Coda

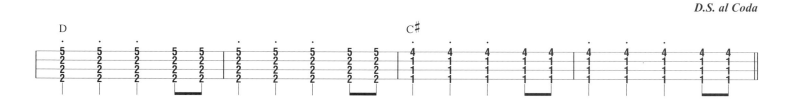

Coda

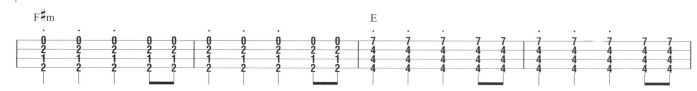

Outro

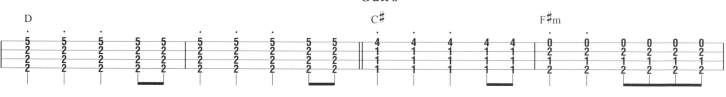

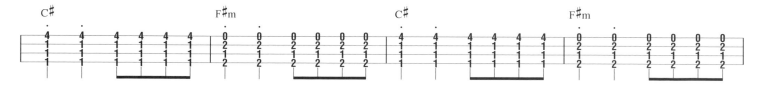

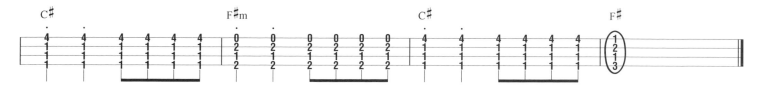

THE MAJOR SCALE

The *major scale* is a collection of notes in a given key that we use to create chords and melodies. Since there are twelve major keys, there are twelve major scales. Each major scale contains seven different notes. This is the familiar "do-re-mi" scale you learned in grade school, and it's the basis for thousands of melodies. In this lesson, we'll look at two different major scales that can be played in open position: C major and F major. Due to the unusual tuning of the ukulele, we'll only be using strings 3–1 for these scale forms.

The note from which a scale derives its name is called the *tonic* (or sometimes *root*) of the scale. So, the tonic of a C major scale is C. We're going to learn the C major scale in open position. Below is the *scale diagram* for the C major scale. Notice that it's simply a horizontal representation of the ukulele neck. The tonic notes of the scale—the C notes, in this case—are circled.

C Major Scale

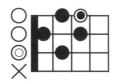

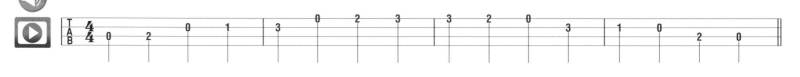

The requisite first melody for anyone learning a new instrument is almost always "Twinkle, Twinkle," but there's good reason! It makes a great exercise and uses six of the seven notes of the major scale. So here it is in the key of C major.

"Twinkle, Twinkle, Little Star"

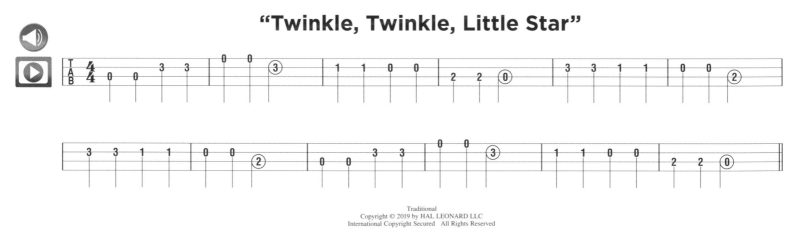

Traditional
Copyright © 2019 by HAL LEONARD LLC
International Copyright Secured All Rights Reserved

Now, let's try a phrase from Simon & Garfunkel's "The Sound of Silence," arranged for our purposes here in the key of C.

"The Sound of Silence"

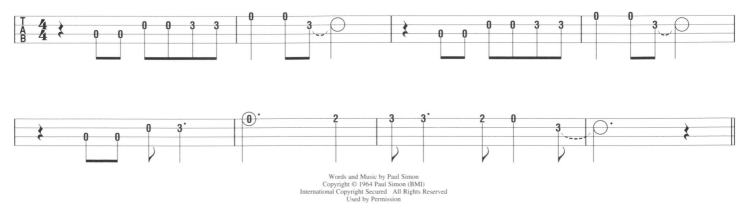

Words and Music by Paul Simon
Copyright © 1964 Paul Simon (BMI)
International Copyright Secured All Rights Reserved
Used by Permission

You may have noticed in our C major scale that the lowest note and highest note of the form was the tonic, C. This is a useful form for many melodies, but it might not work for melodies that span different ranges. For example, if a melody were to dip below the low tonic just a bit, we wouldn't be able to play it using this open C form. That's why we're going to learn another open major scale form: F major. In this form, the tonic—which is circled in our diagram—appears in the middle of the range, so we can go above and below the tonic with our melodies.

F Major Scale

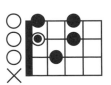

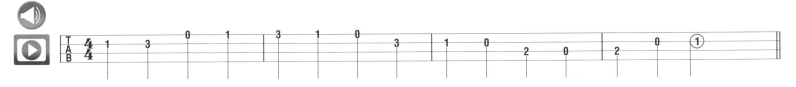

Now, let's try out this scale form with "La Marseillaise," the French national anthem. Note that this is played with a shuffle feel.

"La Marseillaise"

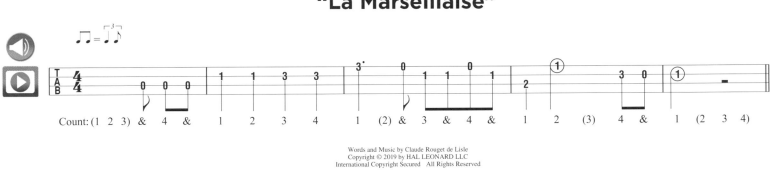

3/4 TIME

For our next song, we'll use a new meter: 3/4. This is the same as 4/4, only we drop one beat from the measure. In 3/4 time, we count "**1**, 2, 3, **1**, 2, 3," etc., with a natural accent on the first beat of each measure. This is also called the waltz meter because waltzes are in 3/4.

There's no chance you're not familiar with "Happy Birthday to You," so this one shouldn't give you too much trouble! We'll introduce one more musical device here: the *fermata*. You see that funny little symbol in the middle of measure 6? That's a fermata, and it tells you to hold the note for an extended amount of time. If you're playing by yourself, the length is up to your discretion, but if you're playing in a group, someone will usually cue the group to start up again. This will make perfect sense when you play the melody, because that's the point at which we all draw out the name of the birthday boy or girl.

"Happy Birthday to You"

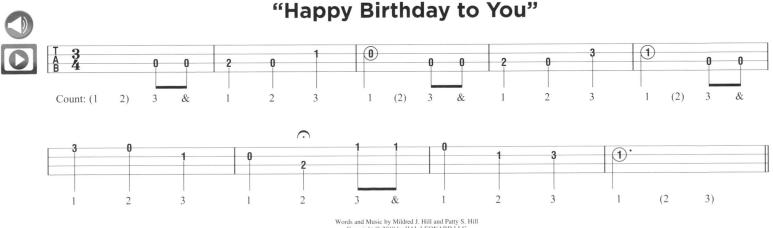

OPEN C7 AND A7 CHORDS

These dominant seventh chords are easy to play and sound great on the uke. You'll likely come across them in lots of songs.

Let's try these chords in a couple of strumming examples.

Example 1

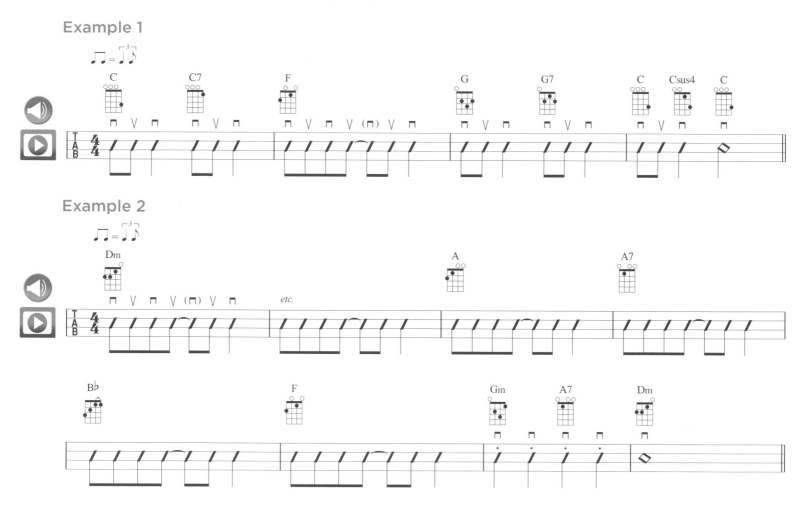

Example 2

OPEN CMAJ7 AND GMAJ7 CHORDS

So far, we've learned several dominant seventh chords, but now we're going to learn another type of seventh chord. A *major seventh chord* sounds very pretty and sometimes slightly jazzy.

These two chords sound nice together, as demonstrated in this next example. Watch out for the staccato chords here!

Example 3

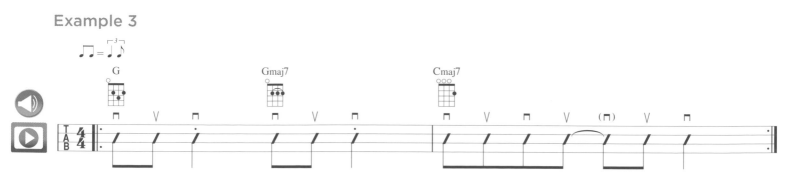

It also sounds great when you mix major chords with major sevenths. Paul McCartney originally recorded the Wings hit "Band on the Run" in the key of C, but we've arranged it here in the key of G, using G and Cmaj7 chords.

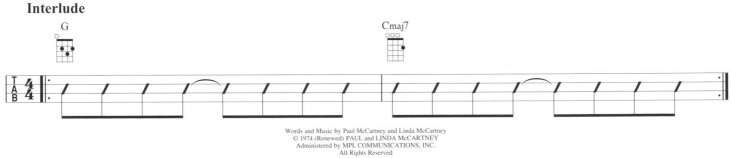

"Band on the Run"

Words and Music by Paul McCartney and Linda McCartney
© 1974 (Renewed) PAUL and LINDA McCARTNEY
Administered by MPL COMMUNICATIONS, INC.
All Rights Reserved

CHORD MELODY STYLE

In chord melody style, we combine chords and melodies to form a complete-sounding arrangement. Just use your thumb to brush through the chords and pluck the melodies.

Example 4

And here's an example in C that makes use of our Cmaj7 and C7 chords.

Example 5

So that's the basic idea. We're just putting the melody on the top string of the chord and trying to accentuate it when we brush through the chord. Let's try a couple of arrangements using this idea. First up is Beethoven's "Ode to Joy."

"Ode to Joy"

By Ludwig van Beethoven
Copyright © 2019 by HAL LEONARD LLC
International Copyright Secured   All Rights Reserved

And here's the first phrase of the Christmas classic "Good King Wenceslas," in the key of C.

"Good King Wenceslas"

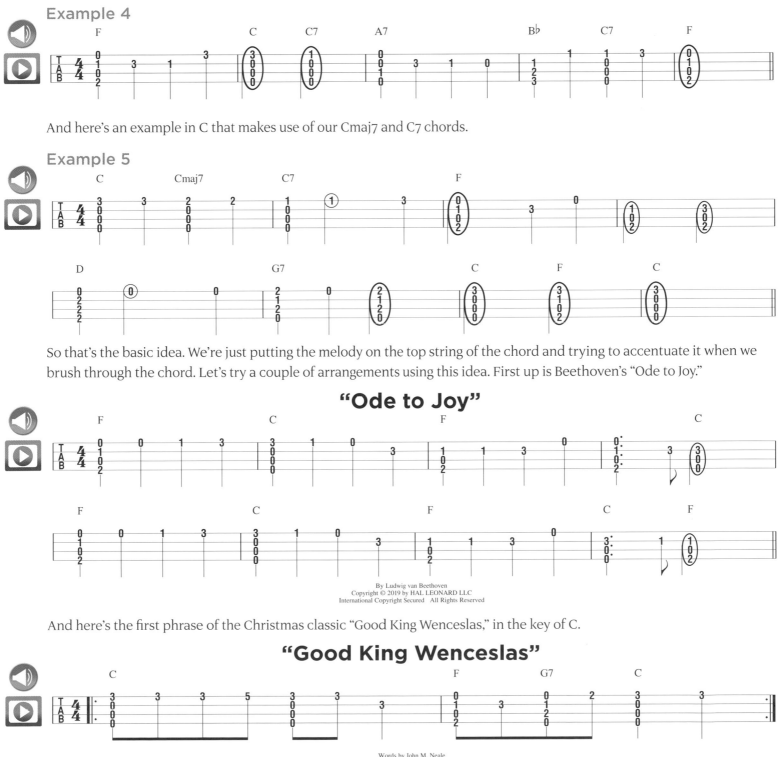

Words by John M. Neale
Music from Piae Cantiones
Copyright © 2019 by HAL LEONARD LLC
International Copyright Secured   All Rights Reserved

THE MINOR SCALE

Just as we use the major scale to create chords and melodies in major keys, we use the minor scale to create chords and melodies in minor keys. When a song is dark, moody, or sad, it's usually because it's in a minor key. As with the major keys, there are twelve different minor keys, each containing a different set of seven notes. In this lesson, we'll learn open forms of the C minor and F minor scales.

Below is a scale diagram showing a C minor scale, with the tonic C notes circled.

C Minor Scale

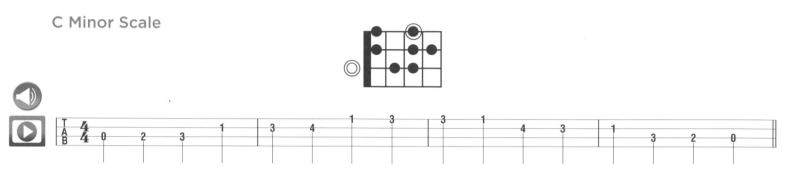

Playing *scale sequences* is great for getting familiar with scales. A sequence is simply a repetitive pattern of notes that you move up or down through a scale. If you think of the scale notes as numbers—1, 2, 3, 4, 5, 6, and 7—you can create a numeric sequence such as 1–3–2–4–3–5–4–6, etc. In fact, let's try that exact sequence with our C minor scale. We're kind of zig-zagging our way through the scale.

Example 1

Since our open C string is the lowest note we can play on the uke, this scale form is often useful when the melody doesn't go lower than the tonic. Here's an example of a melody in C minor using this open scale form.

Example 2

Christmas songs often make great practice for playing melodies, and "We Three Kings of Orient Are" is a minor-key melody that will work perfectly in C minor. This song is in 3/4 and uses all seven notes in the scale (everything but the high tonic note).

"We Three Kings of Orient Are"

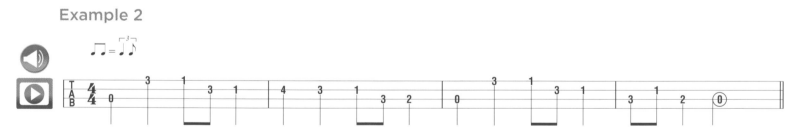

Words and Music by John H. Hopkins, Jr.

Our open F minor scale form spans from low C up to a high D♭. As with the F major scale, this is a nice form to use when playing melodies that dip a bit below the low tonic note, which would be F in the key of F minor. Here's how the scale looks. The tonic F note, on string 2, is circled.

F Minor Scale

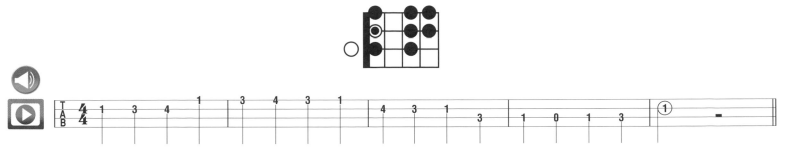

Let's apply the same sequence we used for the C minor scale to our new F minor scale. We'll start from the lowest note of the form and climb from there.

Example 3

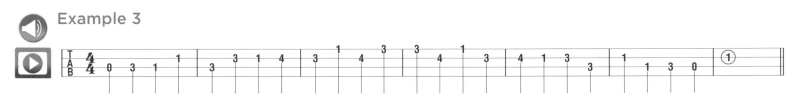

Now, we'll try a melody using this scale. Again, you can pluck the notes with your thumb or index finger—or a combination of both if you choose. We'll take it nice and slow. The most important thing at this point is to try to make each note sound clean. Remain in first position, using your fret-hand index finger for notes on fret 1, your ring finger for notes on fret 3, etc.

Example 4

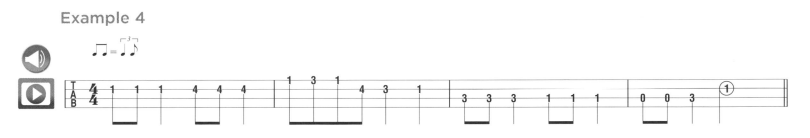

In keeping with our Christmas theme, we'll play "O Come, O Come, Emmanuel" in F minor. This melody uses most of the notes in the scale form and includes mostly quarter notes. Remain in first position again and aim for a steady tempo.

"O Come, O Come, Emmanuel"

OPEN Am7 AND Gm7 CHORDS

The open Am7 chord is the easiest chord you can play on the uke; just strum the open strings! Gm7 includes a two-string barre.

Dm7 CHORD

Although this chord is played in first position, it's technically not an open chord because it doesn't contain any open strings. But it's a great-sounding chord and makes a good fingering exercise because you're using all four fingers.

STRUMMING IN 6/8

Let's look at some strumming patterns in 6/8 using our new minor seventh chords.

Example 1

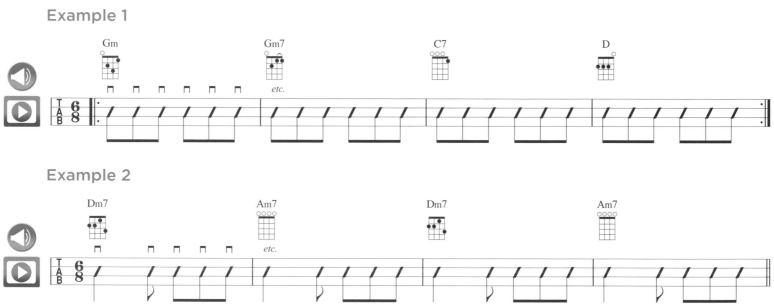

Example 2

MORE FINGERPICKING PATTERNS

This section features several new fingerpicking patterns using the new minor seventh chords. These patterns will introduce the concept of the *alternating thumb*. By this, we mean the plucking-hand thumb will move back and forth between two different strings during the pattern.

Example 3

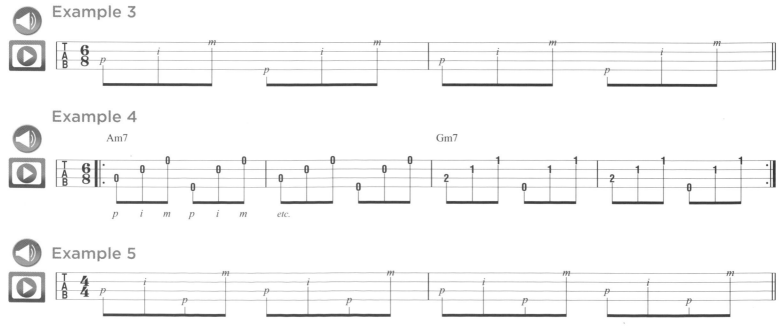

Example 4

Example 5

Because of the ukulele's unique tuning, this pattern—when applied to seventh chords—simply orders the notes from lowest pitch to highest pitch.

Example 6

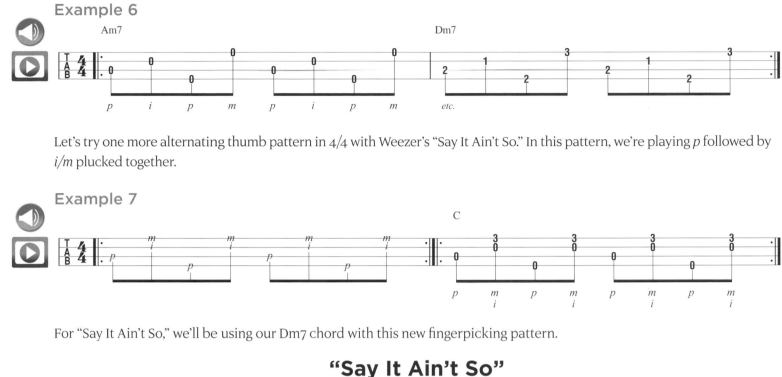

Let's try one more alternating thumb pattern in 4/4 with Weezer's "Say It Ain't So." In this pattern, we're playing *p* followed by *i/m* plucked together.

Example 7

For "Say It Ain't So," we'll be using our Dm7 chord with this new fingerpicking pattern.

"Say It Ain't So"

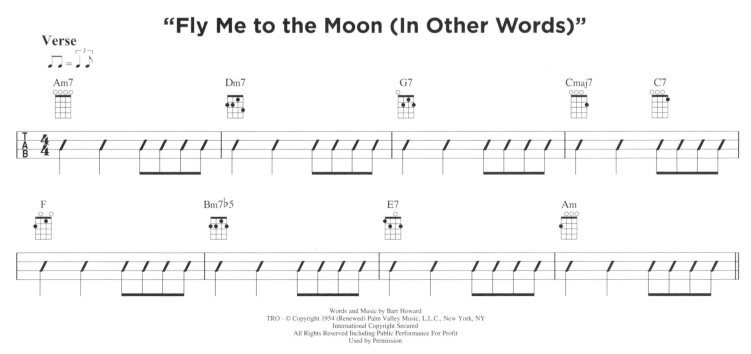

Bm7♭5 CHORD

For our next song, the jazz standard "Fly Me to the Moon," we're going to learn one more type of seventh chord. A *minor seventh flat five* chord is similar to a minor seventh chord, but one of the notes has been lowered by one fret. You'll notice that Bm7♭5 is similar to Dm7; only the note on string 1 is different.

Bm7♭5

2 3 1 4

"Fly Me to the Moon (In Other Words)"

Verse

Am7   Dm7   G7   Cmaj7   C7

F   Bm7♭5   E7   Am

OPEN F7 CHORD

Before we get to playin' the blues, let's learn one more dominant seventh chord: F7. To play F7, we just add one more note (on string 3) to our open F chord. Easy enough!

F7

2 3 1

12-BAR BLUES IN C

The *12-bar blues* is a song form that's popular in many genres, including blues (obviously), rock, country, jazz, and more. It's a repetitive chord progression lasting 12 measures (or bars) and is often made up of only three different chords.

Example 1

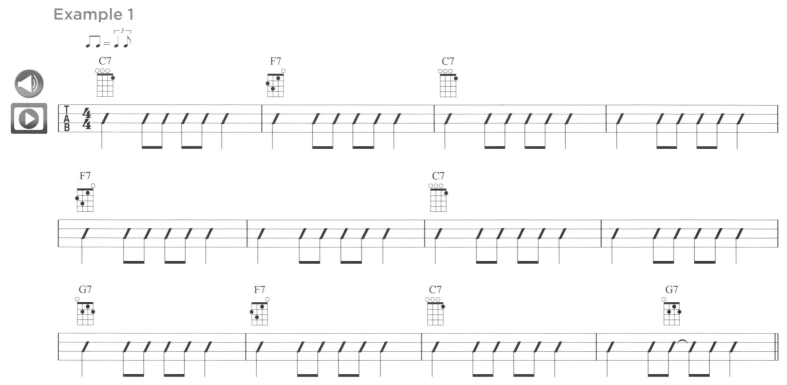

MAJOR AND MINOR PENTATONIC SCALES

A *pentatonic scale* is a five-note scale ("penta" means "five"). The major and minor scales we learned earlier, which have seven notes, can be turned into pentatonic scales by leaving two notes out. If we think of the major scale as containing the notes 1, 2, 3, 4, 5, 6, and 7, then the major pentatonic scale omits 2 and 7, leaving only 1, 2, 3, 5, and 6.

C Major Pentatonic Scale

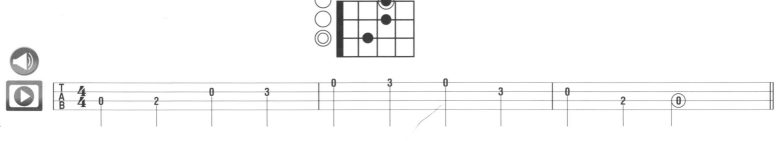

With the major pentatonic scale, you can play all kinds of melodies. One classic example is the Temptations' "My Girl," which runs straight up C major pentatonic.

"My Girl"

Intro

The minor pentatonic scale omits the 2 and the 6 from the minor scale, leaving only 1, 3, 4, 5, and 7.

C Minor Pentatonic Scale

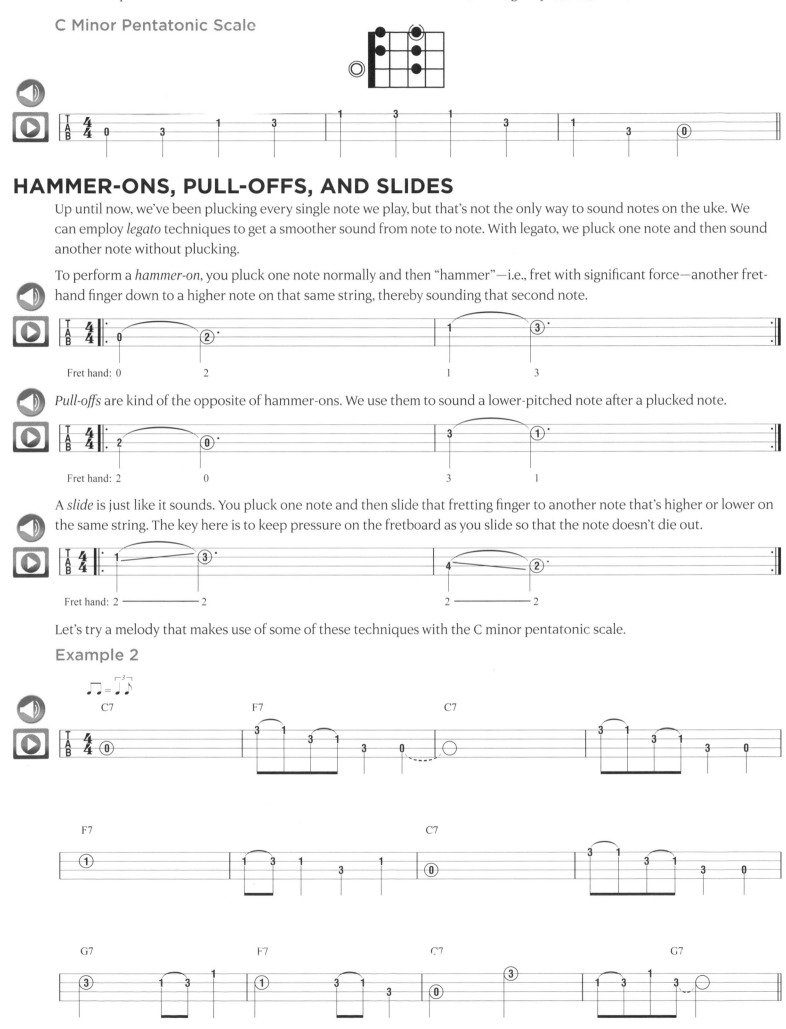

HAMMER-ONS, PULL-OFFS, AND SLIDES

Up until now, we've been plucking every single note we play, but that's not the only way to sound notes on the uke. We can employ *legato* techniques to get a smoother sound from note to note. With legato, we pluck one note and then sound another note without plucking.

To perform a *hammer-on*, you pluck one note normally and then "hammer"—i.e., fret with significant force—another fret-hand finger down to a higher note on that same string, thereby sounding that second note.

Pull-offs are kind of the opposite of hammer-ons. We use them to sound a lower-pitched note after a plucked note.

A *slide* is just like it sounds. You pluck one note and then slide that fretting finger to another note that's higher or lower on the same string. The key here is to keep pressure on the fretboard as you slide so that the note doesn't die out.

Let's try a melody that makes use of some of these techniques with the C minor pentatonic scale.

Example 2

Just like C major pentatonic and the C major scale, the F major pentatonic scale is a leaner version of the F major scale.

F Major Pentatonic Scale

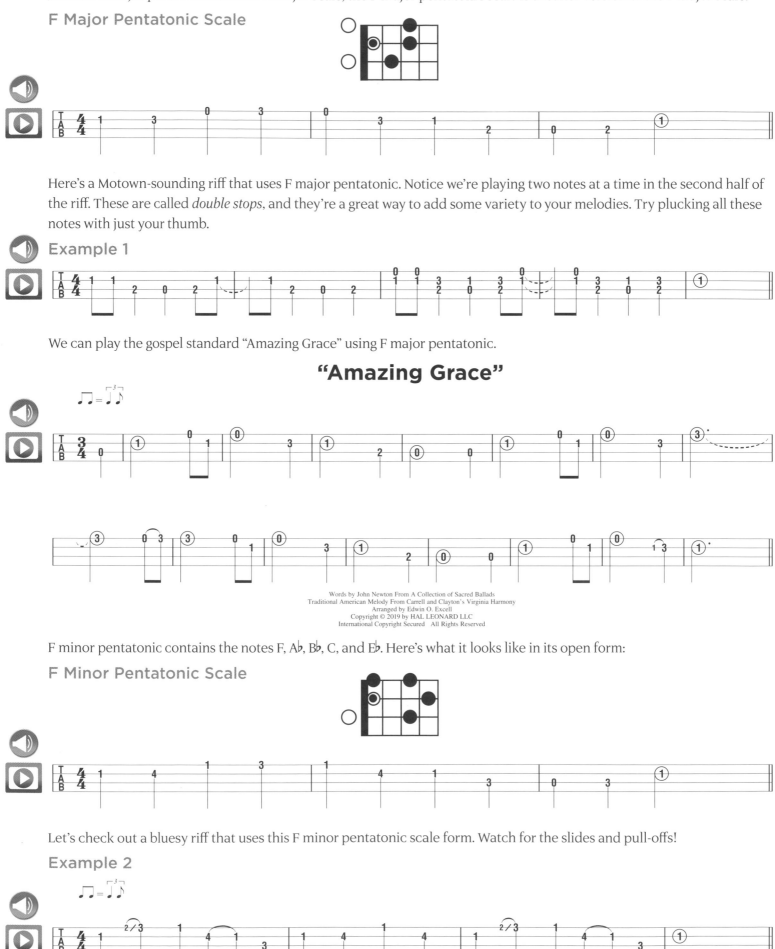

Here's a Motown-sounding riff that uses F major pentatonic. Notice we're playing two notes at a time in the second half of the riff. These are called *double stops*, and they're a great way to add some variety to your melodies. Try plucking all these notes with just your thumb.

Example 1

We can play the gospel standard "Amazing Grace" using F major pentatonic.

"Amazing Grace"

F minor pentatonic contains the notes F, A♭, B♭, C, and E♭. Here's what it looks like in its open form:

F Minor Pentatonic Scale

Let's check out a bluesy riff that uses this F minor pentatonic scale form. Watch for the slides and pull-offs!

Example 2

28

Speaking of bluesy melodies, we can play Gershwin's standard "Summertime" with this form of F minor pentatonic as well.

"Summertime"

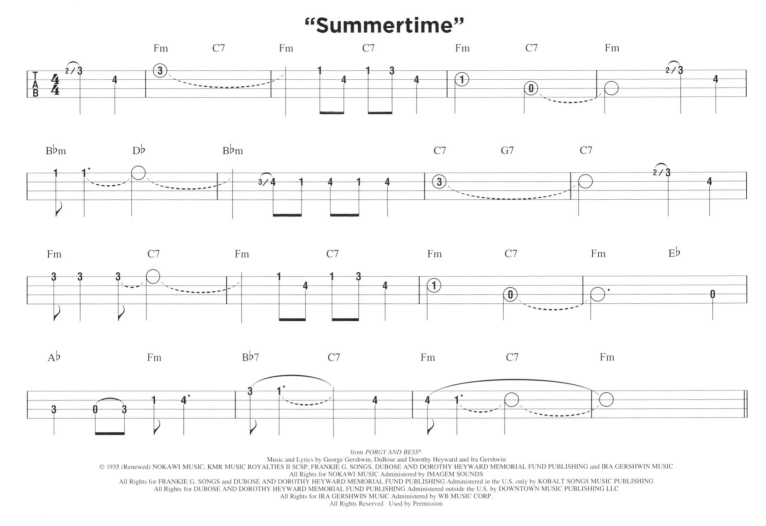

OPEN G6 CHORD

A *sixth* chord is similar to a seventh chord in that it's a triad with an added note; but in a sixth chord, we're adding a different note. Let's try our G6 chord in a short progression, which sounds like a gentle breeze blowing across the beach.

Example 3

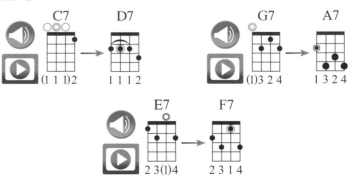

MOVABLE DOMINANT SEVENTH CHORDS

Just as we learned movable shapes for triads in Lesson 7, we can play seventh chords as movable forms as well. We'll learn three movable forms here: C7, G7, and E7. Each chord pair shows the re-fingered open chord followed by a resulting movable chord.

LESSON 15

Congratulations! You've made it through all the lessons. To wrap up, we're going to play John Denver's "Take Me Home, Country Roads" in the key of A. We'll use an alternating thumb fingerpicking pattern for the verses and switch to strumming for the choruses. Also, we'll be mixing open and movable chords with a few little riffs along the way, so watch out for those. Let's go!

"Take Me Home, Country Roads"

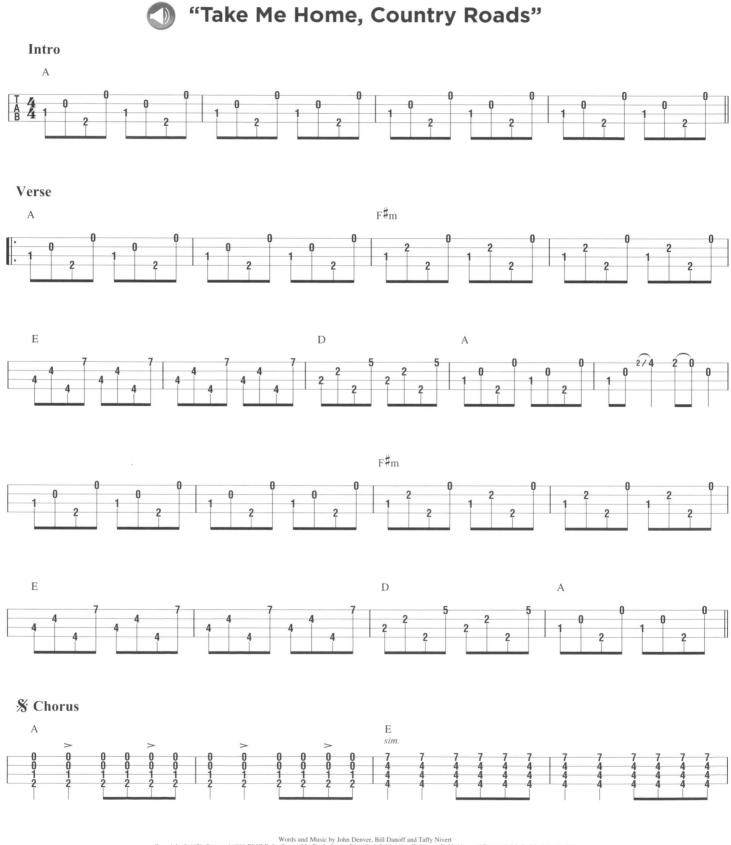

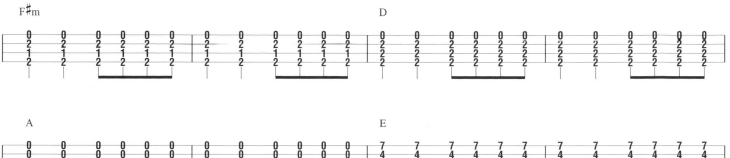

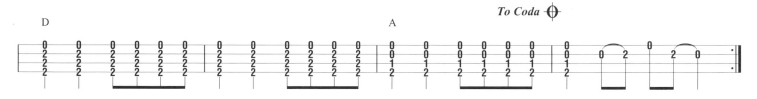

Bridge

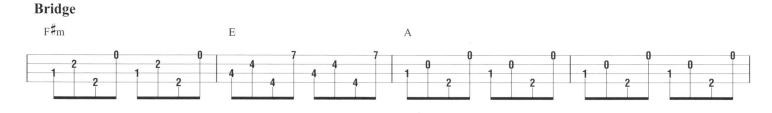

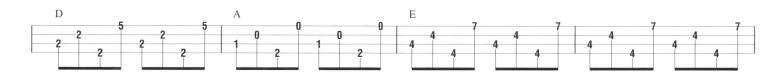

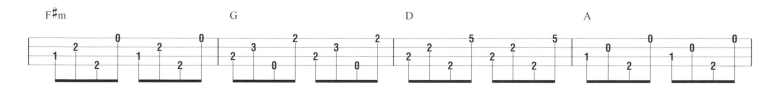

D.S. al Coda

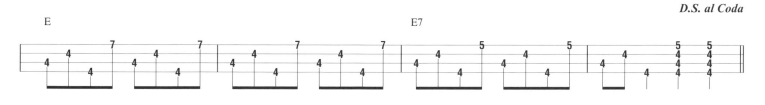

⊕ Coda

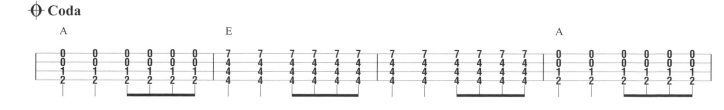

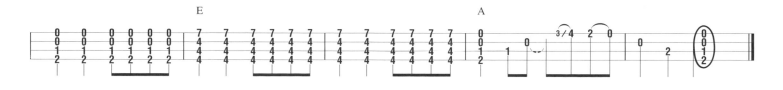

HAL·LEONARD
UKULELE
PLAY-ALONG

Now you can play your favorite songs on your uke with great-sounding backing tracks to help you sound like a bona fide pro! The audio also features playback tools so you can adjust the tempo without changing the pitch and loop challenging parts.

1. POP HITS
00701451 Book/CD Pack $15.99

3. HAWAIIAN FAVORITES
00701453 Book/Online Audio $14.99

4. CHILDREN'S SONGS
00701454 Book/Online Audio $14.99

5. CHRISTMAS SONGS
00701696 Book/CD Pack $12.99

6. LENNON & MCCARTNEY
00701723 Book/Online Audio $12.99

7. DISNEY FAVORITES
00701724 Book/Online Audio $14.99

8. CHART HITS
00701745 Book/CD Pack $15.99

9. THE SOUND OF MUSIC
00701784 Book/CD Pack $14.99

10. MOTOWN
00701964 Book/CD Pack $12.99

11. CHRISTMAS STRUMMING
00702458 Book/Online Audio $12.99

12. BLUEGRASS FAVORITES
00702584 Book/CD Pack $12.99

13. UKULELE SONGS
00702599 Book/CD Pack $12.99

14. JOHNNY CASH
00702615 Book/Online Audio $15.99

15. COUNTRY CLASSICS
00702834 Book/CD Pack $12.99

16. STANDARDS
00702835 Book/CD Pack $12.99

17. POP STANDARDS
00702836 Book/CD Pack $12.99

18. IRISH SONGS
00703086 Book/Online Audio $12.99

19. BLUES STANDARDS
00703087 Book/CD Pack $12.99

20. FOLK POP ROCK
00703088 Book/CD Pack $12.99

21. HAWAIIAN CLASSICS
00703097 Book/CD Pack $12.99

22. ISLAND SONGS
00703098 Book/CD Pack $12.99

23. TAYLOR SWIFT
00221966 Book/Online Audio $16.99

24. WINTER WONDERLAND
00101871 Book/CD Pack $12.99

25. GREEN DAY
00110398 Book/CD Pack $14.99

26. BOB MARLEY
00110399 Book/Online Audio $14.99

27. TIN PAN ALLEY
00116358 Book/CD Pack $12.99

28. STEVIE WONDER
00116736 Book/CD Pack $14.99

29. OVER THE RAINBOW & OTHER FAVORITES
00117076 Book/Online Audio $15.99

30. ACOUSTIC SONGS
00122336 Book/CD Pack $14.99

31. JASON MRAZ
00124166 Book/CD Pack $14.99

32. TOP DOWNLOADS
00127507 Book/CD Pack $14.99

33. CLASSICAL THEMES
00127892 Book/Online Audio $14.99

34. CHRISTMAS HITS
00128602 Book/CD Pack $14.99

35. SONGS FOR BEGINNERS
00129009 Book/Online Audio $14.99

36. ELVIS PRESLEY HAWAII
00138199 Book/Online Audio $14.99

37. LATIN
00141191 Book/Online Audio $14.99

38. JAZZ
00141192 Book/Online Audio $14.99

39. GYPSY JAZZ
00146559 Book/Online Audio $15.99

40. TODAY'S HITS
00160845 Book/Online Audio $14.99

HAL·LEONARD®
www.halleonard.com

1021
483

Prices, contents, and availability subject to change without notice.